Extracting the Precious From
2 corinthians

Bethany House Books
by Donna Partow

EXTRACTING THE PRECIOUS
A BIBLE STUDY FOR WOMEN

Extracting the Precious From
2 corinthians
Donna Partow
with Lin Johnson

BETHANYHOUSE
Minneapolis, Minnesota

Published by Bethany House Publishers
11400 Hampshire Avenue South
Bloomington, Minnesota 55438
www.bethanyhouse.com

Bethany House Publishers is a Division of
Baker Book House Company, Grand Rapids, Michigan.

Printed in the United States of America

Library of Congress Cataloging-in-Publication Data

Partow, Donna.
    Extracting the precious from 2 Corinthians : a Bible study for women / by Donna Partow, with Lin Johnson.
        p.   cm.
    ISBN 0-7642-2696-7 (pbk.)
    1. Bible. N.T. Corinthians, 2nd—Criticism, interpretation, etc.   2. Bible. N.T. Corinthians, 2nd—Study and teaching.   I. Johnson, Lin.   II. Title.
    BS2675.52.P37   2003
    227'.3'0071—dc21   2003006509

*To Margie Massingill and
the South Carolina Wesleyan Women
who demonstrated Sincere Faith
and, in the process, restored my faith.*

*E., I believe in you.
God does, too.*
—D.P.

DONNA PARTOW is a Christian communicator with a compelling testimony of God's transforming power. Her uncommon transparency and passion for Christ have been used by God at women's conferences and retreats throughout North America. She is the bestselling author of numerous books and has been a popular guest on more than two hundred radio and TV programs, including *Focus on the Family.*

If your church sponsors an annual women's conference or retreat, perhaps they would be interested in learning more about the author's special weekend programs. She is also available for luncheons and one-day events. For more information, contact:

Donna Partow
Web site: *www.donnapartow.com*
E-mail: donnapartow@cox.net

LIN JOHNSON is managing editor of *The Christian Communicator, Advanced Christian Writer,* and *Church Libraries.* She has written over sixty books, specializing in Bible curriculum, and is a Gold Medallion Book Award recipient. Lin directs the Write-to-Publish Conference in the Chicago area and teaches at conferences across the country and internationally. She resides near Chicago. Her Web site is *www.wordprocommunications.com.*

Contents

Preface

EXTRACTING THE PRECIOUS Bible Study Series

This Bible study series began the day it finally dawned on me that there were two ways to learn the life lessons God has in store for us: the easy way and the hard way. Personally, I've always specialized in learning my lessons the hard way, through painful life experiences. Sure, I've learned a lot, but I've got the battle scars to prove it too. The easy way to learn is sitting at the feet of Jesus, meditating upon His Word. The longer I walk with God, the more determined I become to learn directly from Him—sitting quietly in the privacy of my prayer room rather than learning as I get jostled around out there in the cold, cruel world. Which way would you rather learn?

I used to think I was "getting away with something" when I neglected the spiritual disciplines such as prayer, Bible study, Scripture memorization, and participating in a small group study. But I was only deceiving myself. The plain and simple fact is this: We all reap what we sow. Nothing more, nothing less. God won't force you to study your Bible. He won't come down from heaven and clobber you over the head if you skip some of the questions in this book. He won't even be mad at you if you put this down right now and never pick it up again. In fact, God will love you the exact same amount. His unfailing love for you is completely unconditional.

But God's love doesn't wipe out the logical consequences of our choices. Here's how Deuteronomy 30:19–20 puts it:

This day I call heaven and earth as witnesses against
you that I have set before you life and death, blessings and
curses. Now choose life, so that you and your children may
live and that you may love the Lord your God, listen to
His voice, and hold fast to him.

Reading God's Word is the ultimate choice for life, not only for us but to those who will come after us. Every moment we choose to spend searching, meditating, memorizing is a choice for life. Every moment we neglect His Word, we are choosing death—the death of our spiritual and personal potential; the death of an opportunity to become all God desires us to be. God's love is unconditional, but His blessings are not. Here's how the psalmist put it:

Blessed is the man
who does not walk in the counsel of the wicked
or stand in the way of sinners
or sit in the seat of mockers.
But his delight is in the law of the Lord,
and on his law he meditates day and night.
He is like a tree planted by streams of water,
which yields its fruit in season
and whose leaf does not wither.
Whatever he does prospers. —Psalm 1:1–3

God says we will be blessed (happy, fortunate, prosperous, and enviable) if we spend more time in His Word and less time with clueless people (my paraphrase). Does that mean we'll never have to learn anything the hard way? Not quite! Let's face it: certain classes require a "hands-on" component. I couldn't graduate from chemistry class without stepping into the lab, putting on my scientist-wanna-be (or in my case, scientist-never-gonna-be) coat, and conducting some of those experiments for myself. At the same time, I found that my ability to conduct those experiments successfully was directly linked to the amount of time I spent studying the textbook in advance. You can't learn what it is to be a parent without having children underfoot. Neither can you fully comprehend God's faithfulness without finding yourself trapped in the middle of a real-world situation where nothing else can see you through. Nevertheless, there is much we *can* learn in solitude and study of God's Word so when we encounter various tests in life, we'll be well-prepared to experience a successful outcome.

Jeremiah 15:19 is a passage that has always been especially meaningful to me:

> *Therefore, thus says the Lord,*
> *"If you return, then I will restore you—*
> *Before Me you will stand;*
> *And if you extract the precious from the worthless,*
> *You will become My spokesman."*
> *—Jeremiah 15:19* NASB

The first time I heard those words, my heart leapt within me and I said, "Yes, Lord, I want to extract the precious from every worthless circumstance I must endure!" I was instantly overtaken with a holy determination to learn all I could from every class I landed in at the School of Hard Knocks.

Those of you who are familiar with my work know I've built my writing and speaking ministry on story illustrations and life lessons gleaned from my various follies and foibles. My friends all tease me whenever they see me embroiled in yet another mess, "Don't worry, Donna. You'll get through this . . . and turn it into a great illustration." And they're right! I always do. But with this new series, I wanted to do something entirely different. I wanted my readers to know that just as we can extract the precious from the worthless, we can extract the precious from the precious too! Rather than telling you my stories, I wanted you to read His story. You can learn to glean story illustrations and life lessons while sitting peacefully at His feet rather than getting bloodied out in the street. Isn't that a beautiful thought?

The other thing I wanted to share with you is this: I love learning from other people, but I'd much rather learn from God. As much as I enjoy reading Christian books, completing various Bible studies, listening to teaching tapes, and attending conferences, nothing on earth compares to those moments when I realize God has cut out the middleman. When it's just Him, His Word, and me, He is serving as my personal tutor. That's when His Word truly comes alive for me. And that's what I want you to experience for yourself with the EXTRACTING THE PRECIOUS studies. I want to get out of the way as much as possible and let God teach you directly from His Word. You'll notice that I've saved my pithy little comments for the end of each chapter, so you aren't biased by my perspective on what's important. You can decide that for yourself.

USING THIS STUDY GUIDE

Every book in this series will feature twelve chapters, each of which is divided into three sections:

Search the Word features a series of inductive Bible study questions designed to help you interact with the Bible text. Use a Bible version that is easy to understand. I recommend the New International Version, but if you prefer a different version (e.g., New King James, New American Standard, *New Living*), that's fine. You may enjoy reading from several translations, and if you're a true scholar, the *Amplified Bible* is ideal for studying a passage in depth. You may want to complete each study in two or three sittings rather than answering all the questions at once. Then, instead of simply copying the Bible text, answer the questions in your own words.

Consider the Message provides a narrative section that illustrates the truth of the chapter, showing how it can be lived out in today's world.

Apply the Truth contains questions to help you apply the biblical teaching to your daily life, along with a verse or short passage to memorize. Depend on the Holy Spirit to guide and help you with these questions so He can pinpoint areas of your life where God wants you to practice His truth.

Although I suspect many of you will be using these books for your personal quiet time, I have included a brief Leader's Guide at the end of each book. It includes some background information on the Bible text, along with cross-references and suggestions for using this study guide in a group setting.

I want you to know how excited I am for you as you begin this journey with God and His Word. You will soon discover (if you don't know this already) that the truths you glean on your own will ultimately have far greater impact on your life than anything you've ever learned secondhand. People died to give us the right to study God's Word for ourselves. It's a great privilege. Make the most of it. As you do, here's my prayer for you:

For this reason I kneel before the Father, from whom his whole family in heaven and on earth derives its name. I pray that out of his glorious riches he may strengthen you with power through his Spirit in your inner being, so that Christ may dwell in your hearts through faith. And I pray that you, being rooted and established in love, may have power, together with all the saints, to grasp how wide and long and high and deep is the love of Christ, and to know this love that surpasses knowledge—that you may be filled to the measure of all the fullness of God.

Now to him who is able to do immeasurably more than all we ask or imagine, according to his power that is at work within us, to him be glory in the church and in Christ Jesus throughout all generations, for ever and ever! Amen.

—*Ephesians 3:14–21*

Blessings,
His Vessel
Donna Partow

Introduction

The Life-Changing Power of Sincere Faith

THE STORY BEHIND 2 CORINTHIANS

The apostle Paul hardly needs introduction to anyone who is remotely familiar with the Bible or the Christian faith. But perhaps we do not know him quite as well as we think we do. We know Paul was a persecutor of the early church—standing watch over the first martyrdom and rounding up Christians for imprisonment. Then he had a dramatic life-changing encounter with God. Afterward, he made three missionary journeys, risking life and limb to plant churches throughout the Roman Empire. We know he is the author of thirteen New Testament letters, which serve as the foundation for the basic doctrines of the Christian faith and comprise half the New Testament canon of twenty-six books.

But do you know of Paul's heartbreak? Most of Paul's writing is triumphant. Even his letter to the Philippians, written from a Roman prison cell, is upbeat—filled with exhortations to rejoice. But in this, Paul's most personal, passionate letter, we see a completely different side of him. We see his frailty, his vulnerability. He's up (paradise), he's down (despairing of life), he's all around. If someone sent me a similar letter in this morning's mail, I'd deem him an emotional wreck. The beatings didn't phase him. It was the attacks of fellow believers that finally *got to him*. He feels betrayed, rejected.

He is deeply hurt by their attitude toward him and he isn't afraid to let it show.

Paul's courageous vulnerability is precisely why this book touches my heart so deeply. He was not some robotic super-saint but a human being with a breaking point, just like the rest of us.

Paul founded the church at Corinth on his second missionary journey (Acts 18:1–18). He stayed there for eighteen months, preaching the Gospel, leading people to the Lord, and discipling them. After he left, he wrote the church a letter (see 1 Corinthians 5:9), sometimes called the lost letter, since we don't have it. The believers, in turn, wrote to him, asking a number of questions; plus he heard news about their misbehavior.

In response to this news and their questions, Paul wrote the letter we know as 1 Corinthians. He dealt with a number of problems and sins in that church, including divisions, immorality, marriage and divorce, offering food to idols, taking the Lord's Supper while having unconfessed sin in their lives, and the use of spiritual gifts.

When his instruction didn't produce the desired changes in their lives, Paul visited the church again—his painful visit mentioned in 2 Corinthians 2:1. Then he wrote another letter that is not part of the New Testament, called the painful or sorrowful letter (see 2 Corinthians 2:4), which Titus delivered to the church. When Paul learned the believers had repented of the sins he wrote to them about, he wrote a fourth letter—2 Corinthians—telling them he would visit them again (2 Corinthians 12:14; 13:1–2). Acts 20:1–3 records that final visit.

We tend to read Paul's letters as doctrinal dissertations. But that's not what they were. He wasn't writing impersonal commentary to strangers; he was writing to friends he cared deeply about, urging them to live differently. In the case of the Corinthian believers, Paul wanted to remind them that serving God is no guarantee that everything will always go your way. And on the flip side, just because you seem to have it "all together" doesn't mean your life is pleasing to God. That's why Paul hammered home the importance of having a sincere faith. The Corinthians already had one of the largest, most dynamic, prosperous Christian churches on the planet. Paul was unimpressed. Are you for real? That's all he wanted to know.

Are *you* for real? Do you have a sincere faith? That was Paul's desire for his friends . . . and it is my desire for you. I pray this study through the book of 2 Corinthians will help you take a few steps closer toward that goal.

Session One

2 Corinthians 1

Sincere Faith Finds Comfort and Confidence in God

SEARCH THE WORD

1 When have you personally experienced "the Father of compassion and the God of all comfort"? Describe the circumstances surrounding that experience.

No one signs up for the heartaches of life, but in the real world, tough times are inevitable. As Christians, we can find comfort in the midst of our pain, knowing that someday God will give us the joy of comforting others with the comfort we receive from Him. Therefore, no Christian need ever suffer in vain. Read and meditate on 2 Corinthians 1.

Read verses 1–2.

2 How did Paul address his readers? Why?

3 If you had been part of the Corinthian church, how would you have felt when you heard the opening to this letter?

Read verses 3-7.

4 How does Paul describe God?

5 Why could Paul praise God like this?

6 List at least two positive outcomes of suffering, based on this passage.

Read verses 8-11.

7 What was Paul's dilemma?

8 What was the solution?

Read verses 12-14.

9 What did Paul boast about? Why?

10 How does Paul's boast compare with what you usually boast about?

11 How does worldly wisdom contrast with God's grace?

Read verses 15-22.

12 What evidence is there that life doesn't always turn out the way we plan—even for apostles?

13 Who enabled Paul—and the Corinthian believers—to stand firm?

14 Based on verses 21–22, list four things God has done for us.

15 What can you conclude about God and His promises?

About God's Spirit?

16 How can God's promises and His Spirit enable us to stand firm, even when plans change?

As Christians, we are always in a win-win situation. When something good happens, we rejoice. When something bad happens, it's just one more situation where we will be well qualified to comfort others with the comfort we have received from God.

Read verses 23-24.

17 What should our approach to ministry be?

CONSIDER THE MESSAGE

In the opening chapter of 2 Corinthians, the word *comfort* occurs ten times, setting the tone for what is to follow. Comfort is derived from the Greek word *parakletos: para,* meaning "alongside," and *kaleo,* meaning "to call." So literally, "called alongside to help." As a follower of Jesus Christ, you have been called by God for a very specific purpose. Not to live out a perfect life in your own perfect little corner of the world, but to come alongside imperfect people suffering the inevitable pain of living in an imperfect world. The temptation for all of us is to insulate ourselves from the world. To sit safely in our church pews and Bible studies, shaking our heads at how the world is unraveling around us. And congratulating ourselves because we aren't engaged in flagrant sin like those godless hedonists. I am always amazed at Christians who devote their entire lives to church activities and never pull their minivans off the freeway long enough to consider that following Jesus means more than running to church to *get* what their family needs.

Following Jesus isn't about getting; it's about giving. It's not about finding our lives; it's about losing them. It's not about being strong; it's about being weak. It's not about rules and perfection; it's about forgiveness and grace. We are "called alongside to help." That's what people are yearning for today. They've heard enough from Christians who condemn them from afar; what they are looking for is followers of God who come alongside to help. Who is qualified to offer such help? Men with theology degrees? Women with evangelistic training? Students with flawless apologetics, who've memorized all the right Scriptures?

> **Therefore, my dear brothers [and sisters], stand firm. Let nothing move you. Always give yourselves fully to the work of the Lord, because you know that your labor in the Lord is not in vain.**
> –1 corinthians 15:58

No. The one qualified to comfort, to come alongside, is the person who has first been comforted by God. And who does God comfort? Those who have it all together? No, God comforts the suffering.

APPLY THE TRUTH

1 Reflecting on your life, what are some of the trials you have faced? How has God comforted you in them?

2 How can you, in turn, comfort others going through similar suffering?

3 Pray right now, asking God to show you people who need the kind of comfort He has already given you. Invite Him to begin sending such people into your life, and be on the watch for them when they come.

As God leads, note the name of one person you will begin reaching out to this week.

> **God does not comfort us that we may be comfortable, but that we may be comforters.**
>
> –aLexander noweLL

4 Memorize 2 Corinthians 1:3–4:

> **Praise be to the God and Father of our Lord Jesus Christ, the Father of compassion and the God of all comfort, who comforts us in all our troubles, so that we can comfort those in any trouble with the comfort we ourselves have received from God.**

You will find the memory verses printed at the back of this book. I encourage you to cut them out and tuck them in your purse. Whenever you have a free moment, pull them out and review them.

Session Two
2 Corinthians 2

Sincere Faith Acknowledges Human Frailty

SEARCH THE WORD

1 When are you most aware of your human frailty? Why?

In a culture that exalts power and strength above almost all else, God challenges us to embrace human frailty—in ourselves and others. And in the typical upside-down fashion of the kingdom of God, where the last shall be first, we discover the greatest power of all through our weaknesses. Read and meditate on 2 Corinthians 2.

Read verses 1-4.

2 What was Paul's state of mind/condition of heart when he wrote this letter?

3 How does Paul's willingness to confront sin reflect the depth of his love for the Corinthians?

The glory of Christianity is to conquer by forgiveness.
–wiLLiam bLake

4 What was his motive for writing?

Read verses 5–11.

5 Paul indicates that there is a time to punish sin and a time to forgive and comfort the offender. What do you discern from these verses concerning this issue?

6 How did one person's sin affect other people?

Forgiveness is not an elective in the curriculum of servanthood. It is a required course, and the exams are always tough to pass.
–charLes f. swindoLL

7 What is the appropriate response to a repentant sinner?

8 What does Paul state as his motive for extending forgiveness?

9 How might unforgiveness enable Satan to outwit us and advance his schemes against us?

It was God's willingness to provide a means of forgiveness for the human race that foiled Satan's schemes at the Cross. Every time you choose to forgive those who have offended you, you foil his scheme for your life. And what is his scheme? To keep you stuck in the pain of the past, so you can't move forward with the rest of your life.

Read verses 12-17.

10 After dealing with forgiveness, Paul switched subjects and wrote about his missionary journey. What happened to his plans?

11 Why wasn't he discouraged when it seemed like his plans were falling apart?

12 Instead of focusing on his plans, Paul focused on God. How do you react when what you thought was God's will doesn't work out? Why?

13 How did Paul's life and preaching affect the people with whom he had contact?

14 Paul said he didn't "peddle the word of God for profit" like other people were doing. How do people peddle God's Word for profit today?

15 In contrast, how should we live and speak God's Word?

CONSIDER THE MESSAGE

In the original Greek, the word translated in verse 17 as *sincerity* or *sincere faith* literally means *without wax*. During New Testament times, clay pots were big business. They were like first-century Tupperware and cardboard boxes all rolled into one—used for hauling and storing everything imaginable. However, since each jar of clay was handmade, it was inevitable that it had some cracks. Everyone knew about the cracks. But since it was big business, the people selling the clay pots would cover the cracks with wax. It was all a game.

In the same way, we have this treasure—the radiance and glory of the living God—but we have it in a jar of clay (2 Corinthians 4:7). Each of us is handmade by God, completely unique. But since we live in a fallen world, where our fellow jars of clay routinely bump into us, some cracks are inevitable. Here's what I want you to grab hold of. *Everyone knows about the cracks!* So why waste time covering them up? What's the number one reason non-Christians give for not attending church? "They're all a bunch of hypocrites!" See? They know about the cracks! They know about the wax! They know it's all a game. That's why it's time to get real. It's time to strip off the wax and be honest enough to admit we're just jars of clay, like everyone else, and we have our share of cracks.

I think it's beautiful how Paul ties together both forgiveness and sincere faith here in chapter 2. There is a vital connection between the two. The pathway to forgiving others is through acknowledging their human frailty. Whenever I'm struggling to forgive people who have hurt me, I ask God to give me the grace to see them not as big, powerful ogres but as they really are: fragile jars of clay. It helps me to consider their life journeys and the pain they have suffered along the way. My perspective is transformed as I realize that their flaws, like mine, are the result of brokenness. Brokenness that was no doubt inflicted on them long before they inflicted pain on me.

Just as we can forgive by acknowledging the human frailty of others, we demonstrate sincere faith by acknowledging our own human frailty. When we discover the grace to forgive ourselves, we uncover the courage to strip off the wax. For years, many Christians were taught that the key to reaching the world with the Gospel was to present a well-waxed image. We worked hard to memorize all the right Scriptures so people would know we had a corner on truth. We lived exemplary lives, pursuing status and success, to demonstrate that Christians aren't stupid. We were, ostensibly, living proof that others would "receive a blessing" if they signed up to follow our God. Meanwhile, we were careful to keep our families in line—little Johnny was the captain of the football team, while Susie got elected homecoming queen. And while we congratulated ourselves on our polished presentations, the world scratched its collective head. That's because people don't need to see how perfect Christians are; they need to see how powerful God is. People don't need to see how Christians never have any problems and never make any mistakes; they need to see how God is bigger than our problems and more powerful than our mistakes.

APPLY THE TRUTH

1 Ask God to show you any unforgiveness you've been harboring. List below people you need to forgive. Now pray earnestly, asking God to show you the frailty and brokenness of each one.

2 What cracks in your life have you waxed over?

> To forgive doesn't mean to give in; it means to let go.... A rabbi who lost his family in the Holocaust told us he forgave because he chose not to bring Hitler with him to America. When you forgive, you reclaim your power to choose. It doesn't matter whether someone deserves forgiveness; *you* deserve to be free.
>
> —dianne haLes

3 Is there someone to whom you need to acknowledge your human frailty? Ask God to show you who it is and to give you the courage to ask that person for forgiveness.

4 How can you speak God's Word with sincerity this week?

5 Memorize 2 Corinthians 2:17:

> Unlike so many, we do not peddle the word of God for profit. On the contrary, in Christ we speak before God with sincerity, like men sent from God.

Session Three
2 Corinthians 3

Sincere Faith Equips Us As Ministers of God's Grace

SEARCH THE WORD

1 What do you consider your qualifications for employment?

What are your qualifications for ministry?

In the "real world," we are hired for positions based on our competence as demonstrated by our existing qualifications. However, as Christians, our sole qualification to serve is that God has made us competent to minister His grace to hurting people. With this in mind, read and meditate on 2 Corinthians 3.

Read verses 1–6.

2 Why didn't Paul need a letter of introduction to the Corinthians?

3 How are people like letters, "known and read by everyone"?

4 Where does our competence come from?

Where doesn't it come from?

5 What is the nature of the new covenant
of which we are ministers?

> **God doesn't call
> the qualified; He
> qualifies the
> called.**
> −oraL roberts

6 What does the letter do (v. 6)?

How about the Spirit?

7 When have you witnessed how "the letter kills"? Describe.

Read verses 7-11.

8 How did Paul describe the ministry of the Spirit, also known as the ministry of God's grace and the new covenant?

9 How did he distinguish it from the law?

10 What was the purpose of the law, "the ministry that brought death"? (See also Romans 7:7–12; Galatians 3:19–22.)

> The glory of the new covenant . . . lies in the fact that it exactly meets the needs of failing but aspiring men and women. It was not given for only the spiritual elite, a holy club. It was designed for people who had made a mess of their lives, and therein lies its optimistic message.
>
> –j. oswaLd sanders

Read verses 12-18.

11 How are we different from Moses as ministers of God's grace?

12 How does Moses' veil help us understand why most Jewish people don't understand the Gospel?

13 What is the connection between the Spirit and freedom?

14 How is this connection evident in your own life?

15 How is God's glory reflected in your life as a minister of His grace?

CONSIDER THE MESSAGE

I was once being escorted to a prestigious event by an impressive couple. As we were driving along in their luxury car, the husband asked me to tell him a little about my qualifications, to which I responded, "Well, I'm qualified for pretty much every twelve-step group in America, and I'm definitely qualified to check into the nut

> As we look into God's Word and see God's Son, the Spirit transforms us into the very image of God. It is important, however, that we hide nothing from God. We must be open and honest with Him and not "wear a veil."
>
> –warren w. wiersbe

house!" He seemed puzzled but smiled politely.

Qualifications have nothing to do with the kingdom of God. Our only qualification is the finished work of Jesus Christ on the Cross. By His sacrifice, He has "made us competent"—or qualified—as ministers of His grace.

Consider the following evidence of God calling the unqualified—even those we would declare disqualified—into His service:

- Jacob, a deceiver and runaway who had to work fourteen years to get the wife he wanted, became the father of the nation of Israel.

- Joseph, a bragging, spoiled-rotten brat turned slave and ex-convict, saved his family (the twelve tribes of Israel and the ancestors of Christ).

- Moses, a murderer turned shepherd—a man so timid he told God to look elsewhere—led Israel out of bondage and to the edge of the Promised Land.

- Rahab, a prostitute—a woman who lived a morally bankrupt life in a morally bankrupt culture—played a pivotal role in helping the Israelites take the Promised Land.

- Hannah—a barren housewife—became the mother of Samuel, one of the greatest prophets of the Old Testament.

- Eli, a man who blew it big-time with his own children (Hophni and Phinehas), became the spiritual father of Samuel, who became the spiritual father and mentor of David.

- David, a humble shepherd boy and youngest in his family, who later committed adultery and murder, became Israel's greatest king and penned many of the most beautiful, comforting, and inspiring passages of Scripture.

- Esther, a slave girl married to a Gentile, saved God's people from an impending massacre.

- Mary, an unmarried peasant girl, became the mother of Jesus.

- Matthew, a despised tax collector and symbol of Israel's oppressors, became an apostle and writer of the first book of the New Testament.

- Peter, a hot-tempered fisherman, became an apostle, leader of the early church, and writer of two New Testament letters.

- Paul, a vicious persecutor of the early church and approving witness of the stoning of the first Christian martyr, took the Gospel to the Gentiles and wrote more New Testament books than any other author.[1]

So the next time you feel inadequate and unqualified to serve God, remember these examples from the Scriptures and be encouraged.

APPLY THE TRUTH

1 Write out a description of your unique service to God *and* your disqualifications (similar to what I have done for each of the biblical characters listed above).

2 Ask God to show you, this week, one person you can minister grace to despite your apparent lack of qualifications.

3 Memorize 2 Corinthians 3:5–6:

> **Not that we are competent in ourselves to claim anything for ourselves, but our competence comes from God. He has made us competent as ministers of a new covenant—not of the letter but of the Spirit; for the letter kills, but the Spirit gives life.**

Session Four
2 Corinthians 4

Sincere Faith Is Willing to Be Broken

SEARCH THE WORD

1 Think about a time in your life when you were heartbroken. Describe it.

What was your initial response to that situation? Why?

How did you grow as a result of it?

No one signs up for the heartaches of life, but in this sin-sick world, tough times are inevitable. God wants us to turn the broken places in our lives over to Him so He can redeem them and bring good out of them. Now read and meditate on 2 Corinthians 4.

Read verses 1-6.

2 What does the word *therefore,* which begins verse 1, refer to?

> **I have been reflecting on the inestimable value of "broken things." Broken pitchers gave ample light for victory (Judges 7:19-21); broken bread was more than enough for all the hungry (Matthew 14:19-21); a broken box gave fragrance to all the world (Mark 14:3, 9); and a broken body is salvation to all who believe and receive the Savior (Isaiah 53:5-6, 12; 1 Corinthians 11:24). And what cannot the Broken One do with our broken plans, projects, and hearts?**
> –v. raymond edman

3 How was Paul's ministry different from that of other preachers? Why?

4 Why do people accept or reject the Gospel?

5 How can you use this knowledge—why people accept or reject the Gospel—as you seek to share the Gospel with others?

6 What did Paul teach about Jesus Christ in these verses?

Read verses 7-12.

7 What is the treasure Paul referred to in verse 7?

8 Why does God put this treasure in "jars of clay"?

> **Will someone be inspired to excellence for Christ because of your life? A broken and contrite heart is a formidable thing in God's hand. His kingdom advances on the shoulders of those who refuse to be put off or satisfied with less.**
> –david swartz[1]

9 List Paul's contrasts between what he and his ministry team were and were not.

10 What impresses you most about these contrasts? Why?

11 How did Paul's attitude toward his brokenness help him keep preaching the Gospel in those circumstances?

Read verses 13–15.

12 What miracle did Paul emphasize in this paragraph? Why?

13 What is the relevance (and benefit) of Christ's resurrection for our lives?

A water bearer in India had two large pots; each hung on one end of a pole, which he carried across his neck. One of the pots had a crack in it; and while the other pot was perfect and always delivered a full portion of water at the end of the long walk from the stream to the master's house, the cracked pot arrived only half full.

For a full two years this went on daily, with the water bearer delivering only one and a half pots full of water to his master's house. Of course, the perfect pot was proud of its accomplishments, perfect for the end for which it was made. But the poor cracked pot was ashamed of its own imperfections and miserable that it was able to accomplish only half of what it had been made to do.

After two years of what it perceived to be a bitter failure, it spoke to the water bearer one day by the stream. "I am ashamed of myself, and I want to apologize to you."

"Why?" asked the water bearer. "What are you ashamed of?"

"I have been able for these past two years to deliver only half my load because this crack in my side causes water to leak out all the way back to your master's house. Because of my flaws, you have to do all of this work and you don't get full value from your efforts," the pot said.

The water bearer felt sorry for the old cracked pot; and in compassion he said, "As we return to the master's house, I want you to notice the beautiful flowers along the path."

Indeed, as they went up the hill, the old cracked pot took notice of the sun warming the beautiful flowers on the side of the path, and this cheered it some. But at the end of the trail, it still felt bad because it had leaked out half its load. So again it apologized to the water bearer.

The water bearer said to the pot, "Did you notice that there were flowers only on your side of the path but not on the other pot's side? That's because I have always known about your flaw, and I took advantage of it. I planted flower seeds on your side of the path, and every day while we've walked back from the stream, you've watered them. For two years I have been able to pick these beautiful flowers to decorate the master's table. Without you being just the way you are, he would not have this beauty to grace his house."

–author unknown

Read verses 16-18.

14 Paul repeats the sentence "We do not lose heart" (also v. 1). What does this repetition tell you about his circumstances?

15 What kept Paul from losing heart? How?

16 How can this knowledge encourage you when you face the inevitable heartaches of life?

CONSIDER THE MESSAGE

What are the broken places in your life? Something you wish were different, something you wish had never happened. You have a choice, right at this moment. You can cover the broken place, or you can allow God to be glorified through it. Here's the way I think of it: Imagine that your broken place is a coupon—like the one you cut out of the newspaper. But if it lies around, hidden away in the kitchen junk drawer, it is absolutely useless. Then one day you make a decision: You take out that coupon, march down to the grocery store, and hand it over with your pur-

> A truly broken person is convinced that God has something worthwhile to say to him, and that he will hear Him out even if values, attitudes, and lifestyle must change. He never feels that he knows so much about living the Christian life that God's counsel is irrelevant.
>
> –david swartz[2]

chase to the cashier. You give it to someone who has the power and authority to redeem it—the power and authority to take something that is absolutely worthless by itself and transform it into something valuable. We're talking triple-bonus coupon here.

That's what God is calling you to do with that broken place in your life. It's useless hidden away in some junk drawer in your heart. Take it out. Hand that worthless piece of brokenness over to God. Hand it over to the One who has the power and authority to take something that is absolutely worthless and transform it into something valuable.

If I had not let God redeem my broken places—my mistakes, my heartaches—I don't think I could go on living. When I think about my past, all the pain I've lived through, the only thing that enables me to press on is the realization that God is daily redeeming all that broken stuff. Even as you read these words today, God is redeeming a broken place in my heart. I figure if what I've lived through can make a difference in one person's life, then it wasn't in vain.

Although I wouldn't wish my choices on my worst enemy, I refuse to live consumed by regret. When a woman comes to me grappling with depression, I can pray with her, and she *knows* that I know. And she sees that I'm still standing, that life can go on. . . . Wow! I can't even tell you what joy floods my heart. When I talk on the phone with a woman who is struggling in her marriage, a woman whose husband is acting like a real jerk, and I can point her to the truth of God's Word—the truth that God himself is her husband—and I hear her, long-distance, grabbing hold of that

> **Broken and contrite hearts are rare. But God loves them. They are the basic raw material through which He works. God treasures every man and woman who lives boldly with a broken heart—*truly* lives. This kind of life is such a rare prize that it is recognized by everyone who observes it. Whether a life is broken over sin, pain, persecution, or service to the Master, people see it shine so rarely that they want that depth of character for themselves in place of the shabby idols of this world.**
> —david swartz[3]

truth . . . that's what it's all about. That's why we're here on this planet. To make a difference.

People sometimes ask me, "How can I know what ministry God is calling me to? I want to serve Him, but I'm not sure how or where." I always tell them: Look to your broken places.

What are the broken places in your life? They represent your most powerful opportunity for authentic, life-changing ministry. It is through them that God wants to shine forth His glory to a darkened world.[4]

APPLY THE TRUTH

1 Ask God to show you the broken places in your life. List them below.

2 Now ask God to redeem each of these and use them to minister to others.

3 How can your broken places reveal God's power to your family, friends, and acquaintances?

4 Memorize 2 Corinthians 4:7:

> But we have this treasure in jars of clay to
> show that this all-surpassing power is from God
> and not from us.

Session Five
2 Corinthians 5

Sincere Faith Understands Its Role As Ambassador

SEARCH THE WORD

1 If you could be an ambassador to any country in the world, which one would you choose? Why?

Being an ambassador may seem like the ultimate career opportunity—prestige, world travel, glamorous parties, and perks. However, when the full responsibilities are made known, not everyone feels equal to the task. When Paul wrote to the Corinthians, he pointed out that we are ambassadors for Christ, whether we want to be or not, whether we feel equal to the task or not. Read and meditate on 2 Corinthians 5.

Read verses 1–5.

2 Compare and contrast our earthly and heavenly bodies.

3 How is the Holy Spirit a "deposit, guaranteeing what is to come" in relation to our heavenly bodies?

Read verses 6–10.

4 What does it mean to live by faith, not by sight?

> **Having believed, you were marked in him with a seal, the promised Holy Spirit, who is a deposit guaranteeing our inheritance until the redemption of those who are God's possession—to the praise of his glory.**
> –ephesians 1:13-14

5 What are some practical ways we can live by faith?

6 One reason to live by faith is the fact that we will appear before the judgment seat of Christ. What is the purpose of this judgment? (See also 1 Corinthians 3:10–15.)

> **Walking by faith means being prepared to trust where we are not permitted to see.**
> –john blanchard

7 What difference should this judgment make in the way we live now?

Read verses 11-15.

8 How did knowing he will be judged someday motivate Paul?

> **We aren't judged by what we want to do and can't, but by what we ought to do and don't.**
> –author unknown

9 How can we follow his example?

10 Why did Christ die, according to verse 15?

Read verses 16-21.

11 What motivation did Paul cite for being an ambassador for Christ?

12 Our assignment as ambassadors is the ministry and message of reconciliation. What is reconciliation?

13 What does this ministry and message look like for us today?

CONSIDER THE MESSAGE

Position Available

- No choice where you will be sent.
- On duty twenty-four hours a day.
- No days off.
- Scrutinized at all times.
- Must be willing to give up personal freedoms.
- Lifetime commitment.

If you saw this ad, would you answer it? Most of us would sprint in the opposite direction! Yet this is the job description of an ambassador, and that's what the Bible says we are. Like political ambassadors, who represent their countries while living in foreign lands for a season, we live on earth for a while, representing

> Nobody can force a single soul . . . to turn to Christ. All that [we] . . . can do, is to lift up Christ before the world, bring Him into dingy corners and dark places of the earth where He is unknown, introduce Him to strangers, talk about Him to everybody, and live so closely with and in Him that others may see that there really is such a Person as Jesus.
>
> —Elizabeth "Betty" Stam

heaven. Ambassadors don't appoint themselves; they are sent by their governments. Likewise, God appoints us, sending us wherever He chooses.

Several years ago, I was raising a teenage girl who was left homeless when both her mom and dad were taken off to prison on the same day. Although Nikki didn't have impressive qualifications in the world's view, she felt called by God to a short-term mission assignment. She was thrilled with her appointment as "ambassador" to South Africa . . . until her plans hit a major glitch. That is, the needed funding was slow in coming. She began to grow discouraged.

One day I brought to her attention the story of Gideon, a young person who also received a special assignment from God (read Judges 6). When Gideon protested that he was unqualified to serve, God didn't try to boost his self-confidence or argue the point. Instead, he posed a question: "Am I not sending you?" It's the same question I posed to Nikki—and one I often pose to audiences throughout North America. Here's a simple analogy: If I were to hop on a plane to Japan tomorrow morning, no one would particularly care when I arrived. However, if the president of the United States were to issue me official papers as his ambassador to Japan and provide me with a diplomatic entourage, suddenly they'd be serving me sushi. That's because it's never about the one who's going; it's about the one who's sending.

Nikki and I put large posters around the house posing the question, "Who's Sending You?" As I explained to her, "If God is not sending you, do the world a favor and stay home. Nothing is worse than a Christian on a self-appointed assignment for God! But if God is truly sending you, go in total God-confidence."

In addition to special assignments from God, we are all on general assignment as goodwill ambassadors to our family, friends, co-workers—even the strangers we encounter each day. You don't have to wait for an appointment in those cases.

Being an ambassador is a 24/7 job, since they are always representing their countries no matter where they are or what they're doing. Likewise, being a goodwill ambassador for Christ is a 24/7 job with a lifetime commitment. Everything we say and do—not to mention our tone of voice and attitude—all reflect on the God we serve. To be truly effective, we must surrender our personal freedoms and private agendas.

One final thought: When ambassadors are insulted, they don't take it personally, and they don't get defensive. Instead, they recognize that the insults are directed toward their country. As God's ambassadors, we shouldn't take it personally when the people of this world insult us or reject God's free gift. People are not rejecting us; they are rejecting God.

Although the job description may sound intimidating, an appointment to an ambassadorship is a high honor and one that offers great rewards. In our case, those rewards are eternal.

APPLY THE TRUTH

1 Have you experienced firsthand God's reconciliation through faith in Christ alone? If so, briefly write your testimony of faith in such a way that you can share it with others. If not, write a letter to God, asking Him to reveal himself to you and show you how to be reconciled to Him. (If you're part of a group doing this study, you might also want to talk with your leader.)

2 Do you sense God calling you to a special assignment? If so, describe what you believe that assignment to be.

3 How can you carry out your role as goodwill ambassador this week?

4 Who in your family, neighborhood, and community needs to hear the message of reconciliation? Make a list and begin to pray daily for each person on it.

Mark one you'll try to talk with this week.

5 Memorize 2 Corinthians 5:18 and 20:

> **All this is from God, who reconciled us to himself through Christ and gave us the ministry of reconciliation. . . . We are therefore Christ's ambassadors, as though God were making his appeal through us.**

Session Six
2 Corinthians 6

Sincere Faith Endures Hardships

SEARCH THE WORD

1 What is the most severe hardship ever endured by someone you know personally?

Very few people in history suffered as much as the apostle Paul, who faced near-death experiences on an almost routine basis. He learned to endure hardships and also how God can work through them. In the same way, God wants to instruct us through the hardships we face. Read and meditate on 2 Corinthians 6.

Read verses 1–10.

2 What warning did Paul give the Corinthians?

3 What does it mean to "receive God's grace in vain"?

4 How can we keep from causing other believers to stumble?

5 Instead of causing others to stumble, Paul endured hardships as a servant of God. What were some of those hardships?

If we believe God loves us and that He is in charge of what happens in the world, then we must receive everything that comes our way as having first been filtered through the hands of a loving God.

6 What Christlike traits did those hardships produce in Paul that should also mark all servants of God?

Read verses 11-13.

7 After Paul described his hardships and the effects they had on him, he turned to his relationship with the Corinthians. What did Paul want them to do? Why?

8 How can we "open wide" our
hearts to others?

**Troubles are often the tools
by which God fashions us
for better things.**
–henry w. beecher

9 What was Paul's attitude toward the Corinthians?

Read verses 14–18.

10 What did Paul command the Corinthians?

11 What were his supporting arguments?

12 What does it mean to be unequally yoked? What are some
ways believers become unequally yoked?

13 When Paul told the Corinthians to "be separate" from unbelievers, he didn't want them to isolate themselves. Under what conditions are Christians to separate themselves from unbelievers?

14 Why is this kind of separation important for Christians?

15 To those who fear separation will result in loneliness, God offers a promise in verse 18. What is it?

CONSIDER THE MESSAGE

We may not suffer the intense degree of hardship endured by Paul, but we all face our share of hardships. Our fellow human beings hurt us in a myriad of ways every day of our lives. They may hurt us physically, committing crimes against us such as rape, incest, abuse, or assault. They can hurt us by "hitting us in the wallet"—bypassing us in the promotion we deserve or overcharging us for products and services. They may hurt us emotionally through insults or abandonment.

Sometimes people intentionally set out to inflict pain upon us. More often, they hurt us because they have first been hurt. I often say, "Hurt people hurt people" and "People in pain are a real pain."

If you examine the interpersonal dynamics in any home, office, church, or community, you'll invariably discover that those who cause the most turmoil are themselves in the most turmoil. If we can learn to deal with them as servants of God, as Paul did, perhaps we'd get a whole new perspective. Rather than focusing on how much the other person is hurting you, turn the tables and ask yourself: What is the source of her pain? How can I help alleviate that pain? How can I bring the mercy of Jesus to bear on this situation? How can I be a channel of God's grace to this person?

As a wise woman once observed, "It's never about people." It helps me to remember, when I feel like a person is causing me hardship, to pause and consider, "Who is really launching this attack? Who is really behind it?" At the risk of sounding like someone who sees "a devil behind every rock," I'm increasingly convinced that the enemy, the Evil One, is behind all human conflict.

The fundamental issue at stake is not between you and "them" or even between you and the Evil One. The issue is trust. Not trusting people, but trusting God. It's about trusting that the God who rules the universe has, in His infinite wisdom, allowed this person to enter your world. Now, there is a point at which you become a "volunteer" for abuse, and that is never God's will. It is okay to remove yourself from destructive people. I am referring here to past hurts and annoying people you are stuck with. Rather than becoming angry with the person, trust God to conform you to His Son's image, to develop Christlike character in you.

Since we live among fallen people, we will surely suffer, one way

> In our society, we have been led to believe that every problem has a solution. We've also been led to expect that every solution is relatively easy, instantaneous, and cheap. But every problem does not have a solution. Even if solutions do exist, many of them don't come easily, few come cheaply, and rarely are they instantaneous. Christians ought to know this, but one of the frightening trends in contemporary Christianity is that we seem to be overlooking this whole issue. We want so hard to deny hardships, the kinds of things Paul says are normal.
>
> –stuart briscoe[1]

or another. Live joyfully among fallen people anyway. Keep this thought always before you: "Whatever happens, conduct yourselves in a manner worthy of the gospel of Christ" (Philippians 1:27). Paul did.[2]

APPLY THE WORD

1 What have you learned from Paul's testimony that can help you the next time you suffer hardship for being a Christian?

2 What can you do to remember these truths when you're suffering?

3 Hardships sometimes result from being unequally yoked. Are there areas in your life where you're unequally yoked? If so, what will you do about them this week?

4 Memorize 2 Corinthians 6:16:

> For we are the temple of the living God. As God has said: "I will live with them and walk among them, and I will be their God and they will be my people."

Session Seven
2 Corinthians 7

Sincere Faith Pursues Purity

SEARCH THE WORD

1 Using the letters of the word *purity,* describe characteristics of a pure life with words or short phrases:

P _____

U _____

R _____

I _____

T _____

Y _____

We generally recognize when people are living pure lives, mostly because they are rare and stand out like blazing lights in our sin-sick society. But a Christian life marked by purity shouldn't be the exception; it should be commonplace. Read and meditate on 2 Corinthians 7.

Read verse 1.

2 What promises did Paul refer to in this verse? (Note: The chapter division belongs after this verse, not before it.)

3 Why should we pursue purity?

Read verses 2-3.

> **Purity is not innocence, it is much more. Purity is the outcome of sustained spiritual sympathy with God. We have to grow in purity.**
> —oswaLd chambers

4 The desire to live a pure life spills over into our relationships with others. What kind of a relationship did Paul have with the Corinthians?

5 How did he express it?

Read verses 4-7.

6 Why did Paul have confidence in the Corinthians?

7 What kinds of trials was Paul going through?

8 How does harassment like this impact our bodies and prevent us from resting?

9 How did Paul find comfort in God when he was "harassed at every turn"?

Read verses 8–13a.

10 How did Paul's earlier letter, in which he confronted a lack of purity in their church body, affect the Corinthians?

11 Why is sorrow over sin an appropriate response to it?

12 Contrast godly and worldly sorrow.

> If your sorrow is because of certain consequences that have come on your family because of your sin, this is remorse, not true repentance. If, on the other hand, you are grieved because you also sinned against God and His holy laws, then you are on the right road.
>
> –biLLy graham

13 What should godly sorrow produce?

Read verses 13b–16.

14 Paul had sent Titus to Corinth to deliver the painful letter dealing with the Corinthians' lack of purity or tolerance of sin in their midst. What might Titus have been thinking and feeling when he delivered that letter?

15 How did the Corinthians receive him?

16 How did his visit to Corinth affect him?

17 How did his report encourage Paul after the latter had confronted their lack of purity?

CONSIDER THE MESSAGE

Several years ago I enrolled in a weight-lifting course at my local community college. And since I've always prided myself on being an A student, I threw myself into the class with abandon. Midway through the semester, my teacher made a comment that certainly got my attention. He pointed out that even though I was working incredibly hard, I didn't seem to be making much progress. Then he posed a simple question: "What are you eating?"

> **A holy life has a voice. It speaks when the tongue is silent, and is either a constant attraction or a perpetual reproof.**
> –hinton

I had to admit my eating habits were terrible. Half the day I'd starve myself; then I'd gobble down some junk food. He suggested eating better-quality food . . . and eating more often. He said it was vitally important to eat first thing in the morning, then every three hours throughout the day. He proceeded to explain that if you want to be healthy, proper eating habits are vital. All the weight lifting in the world is no substitute for the right food.

I think I've made the same mistake in my spiritual life. Maybe you have too. I wanted to do the "heavy lifting" at church, frantically engaging in a ton of activities, carrying the load of responsibility on various work teams and committees. While I worked myself to exhaustion, getting little results, God quietly looked on, posing the question, "Donna, what are you eating?" Sadly, the answer was the same one I gave my weight-lifting instructor—not nearly enough.

Purity comes from feeding on God's Word, living it out in daily life, walking away from sin instead of giving in to temptation. I'll never live a pure life while starving myself spiritually. That's just the way it works.

Have you been playing a little game with the Christian life, seeing how long you can go without spiritual food, then despairing because you give in to temptation too easily? You'll never make serious progress like that. You need to eat first thing in the morning and continue feeding your spirit throughout the day.

Since I've found that planning out my meals in advance makes it easier for me to stick with the program both physically and spiritually, let me encourage you to think about what you're going to eat and to plan accordingly. Your small spiritual meals might include reading God's Word, completing a study in this book, worshiping along with praise music, praying with a friend over the phone, writing out a prayer to God, or tuning in to the daily broadcast of your favorite Bible teacher on Christian TV or radio. Ask God to show you the food that's right for you—then dig in and start eating. You'll find that living a pure life isn't so hard when you've fed your spirit the fuel it requires to produce that purity.

APPLY THE TRUTH

1 Drawing on your description at the beginning of this study, Paul's teaching in this chapter, and other biblical teaching, what does a pure life look like?

2 How does your life compare with this description?

3 Choose one area where you need to pursue purity, and record it here.

4 How can you strengthen yourself spiritually to obey God and withstand temptations to sin, so you can live a pure life?

5 Memorize 2 Corinthians 7:1:

> **Since we have these promises, dear friends, let us purify ourselves from everything that contaminates body and spirit, perfecting holiness out of reverence for God.**

Session Eight
2 Corinthians 8-9

Sincere Faith
Is Generous

SEARCH THE WORD

1 When is it hard for you to be generous with your money? Why?

When is it easy? Why?

Many believers want to give generously when the offering plate is passed or appeal letters from Christian organizations come in the mail. But something happens between that desire and their check-books. Paul addressed this issue in great detail when he wrote to the Corinthians. Read and meditate on 2 Corinthians 8 and 9.

Read 8:1-5.

2 In what ways did the Macedonians show their generosity?

3 What was the secret to their being so generous?

4 What was the connection between God's grace and their gift?

Read 8:6-9.

5 What incentives for giving did Paul mention?

> For the Macedonian Christians, giving was not a chore but a challenge, not a burden but a blessing. Giving was not something to be avoided, but a privilege to be desired.
> —george sweeting

6 How does the use of our money reflect our relationship with God?

7 What riches did Christ give up? See John 17:5; Philippians 2: 5–8; and 2 Corinthians 5:21.

8 Why did He give these riches up?

> **God doesn't want our money; He doesn't need it. He wants our hearts. There is an umbilical cord from your heart to your money.**
> –dan struLL

9 How has Christ's example of giving encouraged you to give more money, time, or abilities to your local church or a Christian organization?

Read 8:10–15.

10 Why did Paul appeal to the Corinthians for their money gift?

11 What principles for giving did Paul outline here?

Read 8:16–9:5.

12 Describe Paul's ministry team. Why did he choose them?

13 Why did Paul send this team to Corinth?

Read 9:6–11.

14 Summarize what Paul taught about giving in this paragraph.

15 The word Paul used for *cheerful* in verse 7 means "hilarious." What picture does that word convey to you?

16 How can you become a more hilarious giver?

Read 9:12-15.

17 What are the results of the Corinthians' giving?

CONSIDER THE MESSAGE

> I do not believe
> one can settle how
> much we ought to
> give. I am afraid
> the only safe rule
> is to give more
> than we can spare.
>
> –C. S. Lewis

Have you ever noticed that the more money people have, the more tightly they cling to it? Two years ago, my friend Martha ate virtually nothing but tuna fish for an entire month. The Atkins Diet? Not exactly, although she did lose quite a bit of weight. Martha's older sister, a high-powered New York attorney, turned forty-five. So the entire family pitched in to send her on a much-needed vacation to Europe. Martha's "pitch" constituted more than half of her monthly salary. Last week, Martha turned forty. Guess what her sister—the one earning a six-figure income—gave her? A sweater. A nice sweater, mind you, but the purchase didn't exactly leave her eating tuna fish.

A pastor friend once told me the fastest way to reduce over-crowding in the pews is to preach a sermon series on giving. Some years ago, I attended an upper middle-class church that was so concerned about alienating people over this issue, they eliminated the collection plate altogether. They put a box in the back of the church and a note in the bulletin with instructions on where to put your contribution.

No doubt about it: money is a hot button. Christians judge each other for how they spend it, argue endlessly over church budgets, withhold it when dissatisfied with the pastor, and donate it to make a good impression or to increase their influence over the church board. We agonize over whether our tithe should be based on our gross income or whether we can get by with a net-income tithe. We listen to missionaries tell of great needs around the world, drop $20 in the offering plate, and congratulate ourselves on our generosity. After church, we go to a restaurant where we spend $48 on $10 worth of food—and don't think twice about it.

Money is a hot button for God too. There are more than two thousand verses in the Bible about money and possessions. That's more than the number of verses on heaven and hell combined. Jesus said more about money than any other subject. He uttered the phrase "born-again" exactly once and we've built an entire theology on it. Yet we manage to conveniently ignore his message on money. If I were to boil it down, Jesus said: put your money where you claim your heart is. It's cliché, but the most accurate measure of our faith is most definitely our checkbook. So pull yours out, right now, and face the truth head on. What does it tell you?

If you're anything like me, you tell yourself that you'll be more generous when you have more money. But all evidence points to the contrary. It is an established fact that the richer you are, the less you give in proportion to your income. In the United Kingdom, the Charities Aid Foundation's analysis of the government's annual Family Expenditure Survey produced the startling conclusion that the richest 20 percent of Britons donate a measly 0.7 percent of their household expenditure to charities. The poorest 10 percent are much more generous, contributing more than four times as much. Here in the United States, a Gallup poll found that households making between $50,000 and $100,000 gave between 1 and 2 percent, whereas families earning less than $5,000 gave nearly 5 percent of their income to churches and charities.[1]

God doesn't ask you to give what you haven't got—but most of us have a lot more than we admit and way more than we need. Let's stop fooling ourselves that *someday* we'll give more. The time to give is now and the amount to give is more than you can possibly afford. Let me suggest a starting point: give so much to church next Sunday that you can't afford to go out to lunch afterward. Remember: there's always tuna fish.

APPLY THE TRUTH

1 If you were going to teach another believer about generous giving, what principles would you emphasize from these chapters?

2 Evaluate your giving in light of these principles. What changes is God calling you to make?

A cheerful giver does not count the cost of what he gives. His heart is set on pleasing and cheering him to whom the gift is given.
–julian of norwich

3 Memorize 2 Corinthians 9:6–8:

> Remember this: Whoever sows sparingly will also reap sparingly, and whoever sows generously will also reap generously. Each man should give what he has decided in his heart to give, not reluctantly or under compulsion, for God loves a cheerful giver. And God is able to make all grace abound to you, so that in all things at all times, having all that you need, you will abound in every good work.

Session Nine
2 Corinthians 10

Sincere Faith Walks in Humility and Boldness

SEARCH THE WORD

1 How would you define humility?

2 Are humility and boldness mutually exclusive? Explain.

People have many misconceptions about humility. They think it means you can never speak up and must go through life serving as the world's doormat. But as we shall see in this chapter, that's not what true humility is about. Read and meditate on 2 Corinthians 10.

Read verses 1-6.

3 What did Paul's opponents accuse him of?

4 How did Paul answer them?

5 What does Paul say about spiritual warfare in this passage?

Humility is not the same as beating yourself up or letting other people put you down. Humility is not the same as low self-esteem and it's not the opposite of confidence. In fact, the truly humble person walks with absolute confidence, knowing that we are simply empty vessels through whom God wants to accomplish His work. When we understand true humility, we understand that it's not about us at all. It's about God.

6 Describe the spiritual war we're in today.

7 What role does humility play in winning this war?

Read verses 7-11.

8 What other charges did Paul's opponents make against him?

9 What do you learn about humility from Paul's response to those charges?

Read verses 12-18.

10 What measuring stick did the false apostles use to measure their ministry?

> **Humility is the ability to see ourselves as God describes us.**
> –henry jacobson

11 What's wrong with their standard?

12 When is boasting evidence of true humility? (Also read Jeremiah 9:23–24.)

13 How can you boast in the Lord instead of yourself?

CONSIDER THE MESSAGE

What an intriguing chapter! In the middle of Paul's discussion on boldness and boasting, he interjects four sentences on spiritual warfare. Are the words misplaced? Was he off on a brief tangent? Or is there a connection? I'd like to suggest that humility and spiritual warfare are vitally linked. True humility translates into total God-confidence as we recognize what's at stake: not our own agenda, but God's eternal plan. Our lives are over—we've been crucified with Christ. So any boasting we do isn't about us; it's all about God and what He is doing through us. If we've been completely emptied of ourselves and are seeking *only* to advance His kingdom, we can be every bit as bold as the apostle Paul.

This boldness translates to the spiritual realm, as we are ever mindful that "He who is in you is greater than he who is in the world" (1 John 4:4 NKJV). Not because we are competent in ourselves to claim anything for ourselves, but because our competence comes from God. I once heard an amusing story about Martin Luther. It is said that one night he awoke to discover his room filled with the overwhelming presence of evil. He sat up, and there, at the foot of his bed, stood Satan himself. Martin Luther looked at him and said, "Oh, it's only you," rolled over, and went back to sleep. Arrogance? No. True humility!

We are not waging battle against flesh and blood but against spiritual powers of wickedness. Therefore, it makes perfect sense that "the weapons we fight with are not the weapons of the world. On the contrary, they have divine power to demolish strongholds" (2 Corinthians 10:4). So what exactly is a stronghold? Essentially, it is a demonically induced pattern of lies that we routinely buy into or which are so entrenched in our minds they've become foundational to our way of thinking, believing, and acting. The biggest lie of all is that we are a bunch of powerless nothings, helpless in the face of Satan's schemes. When we believe the truth, when we understand who we really are in Christ, we will touch the world in a significant way—and we will do so with great boldness.

Since a stronghold is fabricated with lies, the only way to demolish it is with truth. In order to stand firm, we must allow our knowledge of God to have preeminence. We must make a conscious decision to "take captive every thought to make it obedient to Christ" (10:5).

The weapons of our warfare are outlined in Ephesians 6:10–18. As you read the passage, you'll notice that the armor primarily provides a *defense* against attacks. The only exception, the only *offensive weapon* listed, is the Word of God. Although not specifically identified as a piece of armor, it's obvious from the passage that our other weapon is prayer. It's been my observation that the boldest pray-ers are men and women who know God's Word exceptionally well—and incorporate God's promises and precepts into their prayers. In contrast, people who don't know God's Word tend to utter wimpy prayers like "Oh, God, please do what you already know you're gonna do because you know what's best and we don't know what's best and you do. Amen."

If we don't know God's Word, then we need to learn it so that we might pray effectively. We would be wise to memorize various passages that we can use in our prayer times. However, I fear that relying only on short, memorized passages might prove problematic. It's sobering to remember that when Satan came to tempt Jesus, he quoted Scripture (Luke 4:1–13). However, *he quoted it out of context.* Jesus was able to refute him with Scripture by quoting it *in context.* That's why a study like the one you are currently undertaking is vitally important! You are learning to handle the whole counsel of God and keep passages in context.

APPLY THE TRUTH

1 What new insight did you gain about the connection between boldness and humility?

> Not until we have become
> humble and teachable,
> standing in awe of God's
> holiness and sovereignty . . .
> acknowledging our own
> littleness, distrusting our
> own thoughts, and willing to
> have our minds turned
> upside down, can divine
> wisdom become ours.
>
> —j. i. packer

2 How can you incorporate that awareness into your life in a practical way?

3 Spend some time in prayer, with your Bible in hand, exercising the powerful tool of Scripture prayer.

4 Memorize 2 Corinthians 10:4–5:

> The weapons we fight with are not the
> weapons of the world. On the contrary, they
> have divine power to demolish strongholds. We
> demolish arguments and every pretension that
> sets itself up against the knowledge of God, and
> we take captive every thought to make it obedi-
> ent to Christ.

Sincere Faith Acts With Godly Motives

SEARCH THE WORD

1 When did you do something with godly motives? Wrong motives?

2 What were the results in each case?

One of the toughest challenges of the human condition is keeping our motives pure. Even in ministry, it's possible to do all the right things for all the wrong reasons. But we must remember: God doesn't look at results; He looks at our hearts. Read and meditate on 2 Corinthians 11.

Read verses 1-6.

3 What does Paul mean by godly jealousy?

4 What false teaching was Paul afraid the Corinthians would succumb to?

5 How are people deceived in these areas today?

Read verses 7-12 and 16-21.

6 What evidence is there that Paul feels extremely emotional and vulnerable as he writes this section?

7 What does Paul state as his
motive for defending his actions?

**The last temptation is the
final treason,
To do the right thing for
the wrong reason.**
–t.s. eliot

8 When do you think it is appropriate for a Christian to defend
himself or herself to detractors, as Paul does here? When is it better
to keep silent?

Read verses 13-15.

9 What do you learn about false apostles from this section? (Read
v. 20 for additional insight.)

10 Why did the Corinthians have trouble discerning false teaching from God's teaching?

11 How can you avoid being spiritually deceived?

The characteristic of a disciple is not that he does good things, but that he is good in motive because he has been made good by the supernatural grace of God. The only thing that exceeds right *doing* is right *being*.
–oswaLd chambers

Read verses 21b-29.

12 What trials did Paul endure while serving Christ?

13 In what way does Paul's testimony give the lie to the modern notion that following Jesus will automatically lead to a life of "blessing" (translation: comfortable upper middle-class lifestyle)?

14 Another common misconception is that if you are in the center of God's will, your life and ministry will be smooth sailing. Again, how does Paul's example contradict this idea?

15 Notice that Paul tells the whole truth about what it means to follow Christ. So often, we only tell people the advantages. When is it appropriate to tell an unbeliever the downside of following Jesus?

Read verses 30-33.

16 What does Paul suggest we should boast about?

17 Paul says he rests in the truth that God knows he is not lying. What does that imply people were saying about his testimony?

18 Was there ever a time when your integrity was questioned and your only comfort was the awareness that God knew you were not lying? Describe.

CONSIDER THE MESSAGE

Paul did not hesitate to paint an accurate picture of what following God is all about. He didn't try to gloss it over or present a Pollyanna version of the Gospel in an attempt to fill the pews. There's a great danger in the church today—a mindset that says, "Tell them anything to get them into the kingdom." Tell them they can have health, happiness, and the perfect little family.

> There is no better test for a man's ultimate integrity than his behavior when he is wrong.
> –author unknown

It's been my observation that much of what passes for truth today is nothing more than a glorified portrait of what we think ought to be true . . . but it isn't. For example, it ought to be true that if you pray hard enough for your spouse, God will transform him into a spiritual leader. It ought to be true, but it isn't. It ought to be true that if you raise your kids a certain way, they are guaranteed to become stellar Christians. It ought to be, but it isn't. It ought to be true that if you follow God and serve Him faithfully, no one will ever question your sincerity or integrity. It ought to be, but it isn't.

Paul served God with all that was within him, yet his sincerity and integrity were questioned at every turn. Paul could endure all forms of abuse and torture at the hands of unbelievers and rejoice anyway. But what finally got him down was the way fellow believers treated him. Maybe you can relate! I know I can. Notice that Paul makes himself extremely vulnerable in this chapter, revealing how hurt and betrayed he felt by the Corinthian believers. He openly admits to acting foolishly. He says, as we often do, "I know I shouldn't say this, but I'm going to say it anyway." He strips emotionally naked before the world. There are moments when I want to look the other way. This super-apostle! This giant of the faith, who in most of his letters never reveals any weaknesses, here lays bare his human frailty and brokenness. As Chuck Swindoll describes it, "He rolls over like a little cur dog and says, 'Hit me if you will; love me if you can.'"

And I love him for it. Why? Because he has the courage to get real. I can't relate to a super-saint, but I can relate to someone at wit's end—and that's where Paul is as he writes this letter.

Paul doesn't hide his pain . . . but he doesn't let it get in the way of the task at hand either. How many people do you know who, having been hurt by misunderstandings, gossip, or perceived slights at their church, flee to another one? Perhaps you've done it yourself; I'll admit I have! Church hopping is a lifestyle for many Americans. But Paul doesn't let the gossips drive him out. He answers their charges and moves forward. In defending his integrity, he pulls no punches; and yes, I think he may have gone a little too far. (He himself admits as much!) But at the end of the day, we know his motives are pure, even though his words are hard to hear. Yes, he feels rejected, but that's not the point. His deeper concern is the welfare of the Corinthian believers and the advance of the kingdom.

So the message to us is clear: When your motives are pure, stand firm—and don't let the jerks drive you away from your own church!

APPLY THE TRUTH

1 How accurate a portrait of the Christian life do you present to nonbelievers . . . or do you gloss over the truth to try to "win them" for Christ?

2 Which is harder for you to take: abuse from nonbelievers, or betrayal by believers? Why?

3 Is it ever right to leave a church because of conflict? Under what circumstances?

4 How do you know when to stay put?

5 Memorize 2 Corinthians 11:30:

> **If I must boast, I will boast of the things
> that show my weakness.**

Session Eleven

2 Corinthians 12

Sincere Faith Knows the Source of Its Strength

SEARCH THE WORD

1 Describe a time when you were weak spiritually or physically.

2 How did you feel?

Most of us like to operate from our strengths, not our weaknesses. Doing so makes us feel more confident and in control. But Paul learned the true secret of weakness and strength, which he explained to the Corinthians. Read and meditate on 2 Corinthians 12.

Read verses 1–6.

3 What experience did Paul describe in these verses?[1]

4 Why would he be reluctant to talk about it?

5 How might an experience like this cause someone to be proud instead of weak?

Read verses 7-10.

6 How did God keep Paul from becoming conceited or proud after this revelation?

> All God's giants have been weak men who did great things for God because they reckoned on His being with them.
> –hudson taylor

7 How did Paul respond to this "thorn in the flesh"?

8 What did he learn from this experience?

9 What are some of the "thorns" you have had to deal with?

10 How did you respond to them?

Read verses 11–13.

11 How did Paul compare with the "super-apostles" who had impressed the Corinthians?

There is never a shortage of grace. God is sufficient for our spiritual ministries (2 Corinthians 3:4-6) and our material needs (9:8) as well as our physical needs (12:9). If God's grace is sufficient to save us, surely it is sufficient to keep us and strengthen us in our times of suffering.

–warren w. wiersbe

12 In what ways did Paul demonstrate more strength than they did?

13 What are the marks of an apostle?

Read verses 14-18.

14 One way Paul showed his strength was in his attitude toward the Corinthians.

15 What was his attitude? What was he willing to do for them, even though they had slighted him in the past?

16 How can you have Paul's attitude toward people—even those you feel have slighted you in the past—with whom you have a relationship?

**Love is service
rather than
sentiment.**
–john r. w. stott

Read verses 19-21.

17 How did Paul show strength in writing this letter before visiting the Corinthians? (What did he hope his letter would accomplish?)

18 What sins was he concerned might be rampant in the church?

19 What effects would these sins have on the Corinthian church?

20 Which of the sins that Paul mentions here are a problem in your church or fellowship group?

21 How does your church respond to sexual sins versus other forms of sin?

22 How can you use God's strength to make a difference in your situation?

CONSIDER THE MESSAGE

I knew, from the earliest days of my Christian experience, that God was calling me into a speaking ministry. To get an idea of what that might look like, I went to hear a prominent Christian speaker. As I sat through her seminar, I was in absolute awe. She was the epitome of the infamous Proverbs 31 woman: wisdom, grace, godliness, dedication, and self-discipline. Truly an inspiration to everyone in the room. As I walked out the door at the end of the day, I said to myself, "What an amazing woman! I could never be like her."

Role models are important, but I soon learned that God had a dramatically different purpose in mind for me. When I speak, people have the opposite reaction! They leave the conference saying, "What a nut! If God can use a woman like *her,* surely He can use me too!" Of course, if God doesn't work through me in their midst, the second sentence is eliminated and they walk out the door saying, "What a nut!" I've been urged by various people to "acquire a little dignity" and learn to "conduct myself with more professionalism." If the purpose of my ministry were to earn respect or build my reputation, that would be excellent advice. But that's not the purpose. The purpose is to glorify God. And I have truly found that

He is best glorified when I am at my weakest.

I always open my conferences with 1 Corinthians 2:1–5:

> When I came to you, brothers, I did not come with elo-
> quence or superior wisdom as I proclaimed to you the tes-
> timony about God. For I resolved to know nothing while I
> was with you except Jesus Christ and him crucified. I came
> to you in weakness and fear, and with much trembling. My
> message and my preaching were not with wise and persua-
> sive words, but with a demonstration of the Spirit's power,
> so that your faith might not rest on men's wisdom, but on
> God's power.

It is an emotionally risky business to openly share your weaknesses with others. Not everyone will see God manifested in your
weaknesses—they may be too appalled at your nakedness. God
demonstrated this to me in a painful—yet ultimately powerful—
experience last year. I had two events scheduled one week apart at
neighboring hotels in a resort community. The first event was a
complete disaster. In fact, they called my agent to complain, accused
me of ruining their retreat, and suggested I was in urgent need of
counseling. A week later, I again flew across the country and
checked into the hotel right next door to where this debacle had
unfolded.

What a difference a week makes. I was the same person with
the same message. But this time, God came down in a powerful way.
From college girls to gray-haired matriarchs, they stood before me
in tears, deeply moved—not by my brilliant theological insight or
clever how-to program—but by the way God had worked through
a broken vessel. It wasn't about me; it was all about Him. Afterward,
the women campaigned their denominational headquarters to invite
me to their annual international conference. They championed my
cause so passionately that the director of women's ministry for their
denomination contacted me personally to tell me what a tremen-
dous impact I had on their women . . . and to invite me to speak at
this year's conference.

Because I was so impressive? Because I had it all together?

No. Quite the opposite.

Because God glorified himself, not in spite of my weaknesses—but *through* my weaknesses.

Paul openly reveals his weaknesses in this letter. By his own admission, he makes a fool of himself. Then comes the clincher: He admits that God hasn't answered all of his prayers. I can think of a few churches who would write him off, saying he lacked sufficient faith. Some churches only want "victorious Christians" in their midst—and no one who reads this entire letter with an open heart can miss Paul's brokenness. If Paul had an agent, I suspect some would call him and suggest he needs counseling—what with all the emotional ups and downs he demonstrates here. One minute he's despairing of life, the next minute he's declaring his credentials and comparing himself favorably with the super-apostles. What is he? Manic-depressive?

It touches my heart and steadies my faith to know that Paul had a thorn—and God did *not* remove it. Why? Because if the truth were known, every single one of us has a thorn or two. And no matter how hard we've prayed, the thorn remains. But our faith has remained too. We are, indeed, "in the faith." We haven't given up on God, even when He hasn't given us everything we've asked for. And that's the point, isn't it?

APPLY THE TRUTH

1 In what areas of your life do you want to see God demonstrate His strength through your weaknesses?

2 How will you allow Him to do so this week?

3 Memorize 2 Corinthians 12:9:

> But he said to me, "My grace is sufficient for you, for my power is made perfect in weakness." Therefore I will boast all the more gladly about my weaknesses, so that Christ's power may rest on me.

When I Asked God

I asked for strength that I might achieve;
I was made weak that I might learn humbly to
    obey.
I asked for health that I might do greater
    things;
I was given infirmity that I might do better
    things.
I asked for riches that I might be happy;
I was given poverty that I might be wise.
I asked for power that I might have the praise
    of men;
I was given weakness that I might feel the need
    of God.
I asked for all things that I might enjoy life;
I was given life that I might enjoy all things.
I got nothing that I had asked for,
But everything that I had hoped for.
Almost despite myself my prayers were
    answered;
I am, among all men, most richly blessed.

      –prayer of an unknown confederate soldier

Session Twelve
2 Corinthians 13

Sincere Faith Examines Itself

SEARCH THE WORD

1 When has someone warned you about the way you're living or something you're doing/not doing?

How did you respond?

It seems like warnings are a normal part of our lives. Some are welcome, such as signs about a closed bridge ahead so we can turn around and find another route. Others are not what we want to hear, such as a doctor's warning about potential health problems if we don't lose weight and start exercising regularly. When Paul wrote this letter to the Corinthians, he concluded with a warning as well as a challenge. Read and meditate on 2 Corinthians 13.

Read verses 1–4.

2 What warning did Paul give the Corinthians before he returned to see them for a third time?

3 What was the strength behind Paul's ministry?

4 What does God's power accomplish?

5 How has God shown His power in you?

Read verses 5–10.

6 The second part of Paul's warning is the command to examine themselves. Why did Paul tell the Corinthians to do this?

> We have no power from God unless we live in the persuasion that we have none of our own.
> –john owen

7 If you were putting this exam on paper, what questions might you ask yourself?

8 How would someone "fail the test"?

9 What do you learn about Paul's concern for the Corinthians?

> **An unexamined life is not worth living.**
> –socrates

10 Why did Paul write this letter before his next visit?

Read verses 11-14.

11 As Paul closed this letter, what were his final instructions to the Corinthians?

12 What are some specific ways to practice these commands?

13 Which of these commands are easy for you to obey? Why?

14 Which are hard for you to obey? Why?

15 What effect do you think this closing benediction had on the Corinthians?

CONSIDER THE MESSAGE

I used to think the Christian life was a matter of getting out there and getting the job done for God. I thought you found out what you were supposed to do—through a sermon, a Bible study, or your own quiet time—and then you did it. If you did a good job, God would be proud of you. If you blew it (and, of course, I almost always blew it), He'd lower the heavenly hammer.

Actually, that's what most religions boil down to. We perform on earth's stage while God watches passively, rating us on a scale of one to ten. Some of the most popular religions teach that God grades on a curve. That is to say, as long as you're not much worse than everyone else, you should be able to slip into heaven. However, all such performance-based religions are man-made.

Genuine Christianity is not about performance; it's about a relationship. It's about the God of the universe reaching down and initiating a personal love relationship with sinful people like you and me. Whether or not we have that relationship is the bottom line of the exam Paul told the Corinthians to take as part of his warning to them.

Once we pass that exam, the next part is whether or not our daily lives reflect an ongoing love relationship with God, which Jesus talked about in John 15. When we bear fruit as a natural extension of our life in Christ, it is to the Father's glory. And why does God want us to bring Him glory? Is it a heavenly ego trip? No! He wants people to see that we are His disciples so they too will desire to become His disciples. We may not think it's the most efficient method, but this is the method God has chosen to reach the world.

The whole reason God created you and me is so we might reflect His glory and enjoy a love relationship with Him. When we go about doing great things for God in our own strength, we rob God of His glory. Far from being pleased with us, Jesus says the Father will cut us off. The last thing God needs is another glory-seeker in the church; Satan has already planted enough of those in strategic places.

If we want to bear fruit, we must examine our relationship with God to be sure we have one and, assuming it's genuine, remain in close fellowship with Christ. He is the source of life. The moment we walk away and start working as independent contractors, we have cut ourselves off from the very source of our lives. That's what Paul wanted to be sure the Corinthians didn't do and what Jesus emphasized to His disciples—and us.

> **The man who does not like self-examination may be pretty certain that things need examining.**
> –c. h. spurgeon

Jesus promised that as long as we remain in Him, we will

produce fruit and remain in the Father's love (John 15:5). And the world will see God's power in us, just as the Corinthians saw it in Paul.[1]

APPLY THE TRUTH

1 Review the goals toward spiritual maturity that Paul gave the Corinthians as he ended this letter. Which one do you want to work on this week?

2 What practical, specific steps can you take to achieve that goal?

3 Memorize 2 Corinthians 13:11:

> **Finally, brothers, good-by. Aim for perfection, listen to my appeal, be of one mind, live in peace. And the God of love and peace will be with you.**

Leader's Guide

TO ENCOURAGE GROUP DISCUSSION

- If your group isn't used to discussing together, explain at the beginning of the first session that these studies are designed for discussion, not lecture. Encourage each member to participate, but keep in mind that it may take several meetings before shy members feel comfortable enough to participate.
- Encourage discussion by asking several people to contribute answers to a question. "What do the rest of you think?" or "Is there anything else that could be added?" are two ways of doing this.
- Receive all contributions warmly. Never bluntly reject what anyone says, even if you think the answer is incorrect. Instead, ask what others think and/or ask the person to identify the verse(s) that led her to that conclusion.
- Be sure you don't talk too much as the leader. Redirect questions that you are asked. A discussion should move in the form of a bouncing ball, back and forth between members, not in the form of a fan with the discussion always coming back to the leader at that point. The leader acts as a moderator. As members of a group get to know one another better, the discussion will move more freely.
- Don't be afraid of pauses or long silences. People need time to think about the questions. Never answer your own question—either rephrase it or move on to another area for discussion.
- Watch hesitant members for an indication by facial expression or body language that they have something to say, and then give them an encouraging nod or speak their names.
- Discourage too-talkative members from monopolizing the discussion by specifically directing questions to others. If necessary,

speak to them privately about the need for discussion and enlist their help in encouraging everyone to participate.

- End the sessions by praying for one another, thanking God for growth, and asking Him for help to practice the truth discovered during the week. Vary the prayer times by staying together, breaking into smaller groups or pairs, using sentence prayers, etc. Resist the ever-present temptation to spend more time talking about prayer than actually praying. When it's time to pray, don't waste time on elaborate prayer requests for Susie's uncle's cousin's neighbor's grandmother. Instead, allow the Holy Spirit to bring forth what is on His heart as He prompts individual members to pray.

DISCUSSION LEADER'S NOTES

1: Sincere Faith Finds Comfort and Confidence in God: 2 Corinthians 1

Purpose: To identify ways to share God's comfort with others and increase confidence in God.

Question 1: Each study begins with an icebreaker question such as this one. Ask a few volunteers to share their answers. As your group members get to know one another better, you may want to go around the circle and have everyone respond to this opening question. Pray for sensitivity in how you use it so you don't embarrass anyone or put people on the spot.

Question 2: Review the background information on this letter in the introduction to this guide. You may want to do additional background reading in a commentary or two.

Question 7: Asia was Paul's headquarters for his missionary journeys. It is now western Turkey.

"In our hearts we felt the sentence of death" (v. 9) indicates that Paul had accepted the call to martyrdom, if necessary, for the spread of the Gospel. This sentence brings to mind a condemned person carrying the written instructions for his execution as he walked to his death on a cross.

Question 14: The Holy Spirit as the "deposit" (v. 22) is a business term that relates to a sale. He is the down payment or first installment that guarantees God will finish our salvation: give us eternal life in heaven. He is also God's seal, indicating that we belong to Him. A seal or stamp was placed in hot wax to seal documents or jars filled with merchandise as a security measure and indication of ownership. Likewise, the Holy Spirit living in us signifies God's ownership and security.

2: Sincere Faith Acknowledges Human Frailty: 2 Corinthians 2

Purpose: To embrace our weaknesses to experience God's power.

Question 6: We don't know if the person Paul mentioned here is the same one as in 1 Corinthians 5 or not. Whatever the sin was, the church had disciplined him for it, and he repented.

Question 11: Be prepared to share your own reactions, especially if no one volunteers to answer this question (and similar ones throughout this study guide).

Question 14: The word *peddle* relates to a huckster for whom the sale is all-important, who uses showmanship and salesmanship to the point of being dishonest, and for whom the end justifies the means.

3: Sincere Faith Equips Us As Ministers of God's Grace: 2 Corinthians 3

Purpose: To become more like Christ in order to better minister His grace to others.

Question 2: Travelers often carried letters of recommendation with them to prove to others that they could be trusted and given lodging. Other mentions of these letters are in Acts 18:27, Romans 16:1–2, and 1 Corinthians 16:3. You may want to ask volunteers to read these verses.

Question 3: If you have time, ask volunteers to read Exodus 31:18; Jeremiah 31:33; and Ezekiel 11:19–21; 36:26–27. Discuss how the images of 2 Corinthians 3:2–3 compare with these.

Question 10: Take the time to have group members look up these cross-references to add to your understanding of this question.

4: Sincere Faith Is Willing to Be Broken: 2 Corinthians 4

Purpose: To ask God to redeem the broken places of life and use them to show His power to others.

Question 2: This is a good place to remind group members to look beyond chapter and verse divisions. The word *therefore* links verse 1 to the content before this chapter.

Question 3: The word *distort* in verse 2 refers to a practice by merchants who sometimes mixed cheaper substances or goods with more expensive ones in order to cheat their customers. The word was also used of speakers who were more concerned about their delivery than their content. Paul denied this charge against himself.

Question 4: Follow up by asking: Who is the "god of this age" and what is he capable of doing to unbelievers?

Question 8: Clay jars were cheap, fragile, and disposable if cracked or broken, unlike valuable bronze ones.

Question 9: Note that the word *are* is present tense. So often Christians want to pretend that we only had problems a long time ago, but now that we are following Jesus our problems are solved. Paul isn't afraid to admit that he still has problems even though he loves and serves God.

Question 16: Notice the progression from grace to thanksgiving to glory. Ask volunteers to tell how they have seen that progression in their own life or in the lives of fellow believers.

5: Sincere Faith Understands Its Role As Ambassador: 2 Corinthians 5

Purpose: To recognize that God has called us to be His ambassadors and to look for ways to carry out that role.

Question 6: In Corinth, the *bema,* or judgment seat, was a raised platform from which public proclamations were made and city officials announced judges' sentencings. Ask a volunteer to read the cross-reference. Be sure your group members understand that this judgment is based on our works after salvation; it does not determine whether or not we are saved. Salvation is based on faith in Christ, not works; see Ephesians 2:8–10.

Question 12: The Greek word translated "reconcile" literally means to change or exchange, especially money. When used in reference to people, it means to change from being enemies to friends. In the context of the relationship between God and man, reconciliation is something God accomplishes through the death of His Son as a substitutionary sacrifice for our sins. People are reconciled to God when they change their attitude toward Him and accept His provision through faith in Christ. See Romans 5:10.

6: Sincere Faith Endures Hardships: 2 Corinthians 6

Purpose: To realize God allows hardships in our lives so we can become more like Christ.

Questions 5 and 6: It was common for philosophers to relate their hardships as proof of their commitments and sincerity of messages. They also described themselves by their virtues so their readers would see them as role models to emulate. True teachers had to stress their motives and actions to distinguish themselves from false teachers, which Paul did here.

Question 12: Paul's use of the phrase "yoked together" in verse 14 is based on yoking two animals together to pull a plow. If two different kinds of animals are yoked together, forming an unequal yoke, the weaker one will suffer as they pull.

Question 14: For more teaching on separation, read 1 John 2:15–17 and 1 Corinthians 5:11. Ask: How can we reconcile our role as ambassadors with Paul's exhortation to "come out and be separate"?

7: Sincere Faith Pursues Purity: 2 Corinthians 7

Purpose: To desire to pursue a pure life, including confronting sin.

Question 1: The Greek word for "purify" means to cleanse, make free from mixing in anything unclean.

Question 11: Repentance (v. 9) means a change of mind and heart, to turn around, to turn from sin and to God.

Question 12: Sorrow that leads to repentance is the appropriate response to sin, a godly sorrow. But if it only produces regret and not repentance, it is worldly sorrow.

8: Sincere Faith Is Generous: 2 Corinthians 8–9

Purpose: To evaluate current giving practices in light of Paul's teaching on this topic.

Question 4: When we begin to understand what it cost God to provide our salvation, it's easy to give our money back to Him in a generous way.

Question 7: Ask volunteers to read the cross-references to help your group members understand what Christ gave up.

Question 14: Paul emphasized that giving for believers is voluntary, since people were often forced to give to support public projects, sometimes resulting in bankruptcy.

Question 17: Verse 15 refers to the time when God provided daily manna for the Israelites to eat in the wilderness. Everyone had just enough; those who hoarded more lost it through spoiling. See Exodus 16:11–20.

9: Sincere Faith Walks in Humility and Boldness: 2 Corinthians 10

Purpose: To learn to act with humility, instead of pride.

Question 5: The Greek word for "punish" in verse 6 is a legal term that means both to take vengeance and do justice. It indicates a just punishment, not a punitive one.

For more details on the spiritual war we're in and the weapons we have to fight with, read Ephesians 6:10–18.

Question 8: Paul's statement in verse 7 is reinforced in Acts 26:12–18 and Galatians 1:11–12.

10: Sincere Faith Acts With Godly Motives: 2 Corinthians 11

Purpose: To practice acting with godly motives.

Question 3: You might want to ask group members to contrast their jealousy with Paul's.

Question 5: Although it will be easy for group members to name multiple spiritual deceptions, don't spend too much time on this question.

Question 12: Most people boasted in their accomplishments or heritage, not in their sufferings. When they did boast in sufferings, it was to prove how strong they were. Paul, on the other hand, listed his sufferings to prove his weakness, which, in the spiritual realm, is strength.

Question 15: Travel in Paul's day was a dangerous venture, as he summarizes here. People didn't travel for pleasure, only for business or necessity. When they did travel, they took care of their affairs before leaving and went in groups for protection.

11: Sincere Faith Knows the Source of Its Strength: 2 Corinthians 12

Purpose: To desire to let God demonstrate His strength through our weakness.

Question 6: We don't know what Paul's "thorn in the flesh" was. Some commentators think it was an eye disease, based on Galatians 6:11.

Teachers in Paul's day solicited financial support, charged fees, or begged. They did not work at manual labor to support themselves. Paul's job as a tentmaker was an embarrassment to the Corinthian church.

Question 17: Review the chronology of Paul's letters and visits from the introduction to this guide.

Question 21: Ask the Spirit for sensitivity about whether or not to discuss this question in the group and, if so, how to handle it.

12: Sincere Faith Examines Itself: 2 Corinthians 13

Purpose: To grow toward spiritual maturity.

Question 3: Paul majored on God's power in weakness because the Corinthians and their society valued power that brought attention to people, not God.

Question 5: Don't let group members eat up a lot of study time here. Instruct them to keep their stories short.

Question 6: For tests of genuine conversion, see Romans 8:9, 16; 1 John 2:29; 3:9, 14; 5:4.

Question 15: Paul mentioned the Trinity in his closing benediction in verse 14. For more passages on the Trinity, read Matthew 3:16–17; John 14:15–17; 1 Corinthians 12:3–6; 2 Thessalonians 2:13; and 1 Peter 1:1–2. Based on these passages, describe each person of the Trinity.

Endnotes

Session Three
1. Adapted from *Becoming a Vessel God Can Use* (Minneapolis: Bethany House Publishers, 1996), 30–32.

Session Four
1. David Swartz, *Dancing With Broken Bones* (Colorado Springs: NavPress, 1987), 141.
2. Ibid., 136.
3. Ibid., 142.
4. Adapted from *Living in Absolute Freedom* (Minneapolis: Bethany House Publishers, 2000), 150–151.

Session Six
1. Stuart Briscoe, *How to Be a Motivated Christian* (Wheaton, Ill.: Victor Books, 1987), 138.
2. Adapted from *Standing Firm* (Minneapolis: Bethany House Publishers, 2001), 186–88.

Session Seven
1. Adapted from *Standing Firm*, 62–64.

Session Eight
1. Obtained from the Internet.

Session Eleven
1. It was common for rabbis to speak about themselves in third person as Paul did here.

Session Twelve
1. Adapted from *Becoming a Vessel God Can Use* (Minneapolis: Bethany House Publishers, 1996), 225–26.

Bibliography

Hafemann, Scott J. *2 Corinthians (The NIV Application Commentary)*. Grand Rapids, Mich.: Zondervan, 2000.

Kent, Jr., Homer A. *A Heart Opened Wide: Studies in 2 Corinthians*. Grand Rapids, Mich.: Baker Book House, 1982

Life Application Bible Commentary: 1 & 2 Corinthians. Wheaton, Ill.: Victor Books, 1984.

4. *Sincere Faith Is Willing to Be Broken*

2 Corinthians 4:7

But we have this treasure in jars of clay to show that this all-surpassing power is from God and not from us.

---

1. *Sincere Faith Finds Comfort and Confidence in God*

2 Corinthians 1:3–4

Praise be to the God and Father of our Lord Jesus Christ, the Father of compassion and the God of all comfort, who comforts us in all our troubles, so that we can comfort those in any trouble with the comfort we ourselves have received from God.

---

5. *Sincere Faith Understands Its Role As Ambassador*

2 Corinthians 5:18, 20

All this is from God, who reconciled us to himself through Christ and gave us the ministry of reconciliation. . . . We are therefore Christ's ambassadors, as though God were making his appeal through us.

---

2. *Sincere Faith Acknowledges Human Frailty*

2 Corinthians 2:17

Unlike so many, we do not peddle the word of God for profit. On the contrary, in Christ we speak before God with sincerity, like men sent from God.

---

6. *Sincere Faith Endures Hardships*

2 Corinthians 6:16

For we are the temple of the living God. As God has said: "I will live with them and walk among them, and I will be their God, and they will be my people."

---

3. *Sincere Faith Equips Us As Ministers of God's Grace*

2 Corinthians 3:5–6

Not that we are competent in ourselves to claim anything for ourselves, but our competence comes from God. He has made us competent as ministers of a new covenant—not of the letter but of the Spirit; for the letter kills, but the Spirit gives life.

10. *Sincere Faith Acts With Godly Motives*

2 Corinthians 11:30

If I must boast, I will boast of the things that show my weakness.

---

7. *Sincere Faith Pursues Purity*

2 Corinthians 7:1

Since we have these promises, dear friends, let us purify ourselves from everything that contaminates body and spirit, perfecting holiness out of reverence for God.

---

11. *Sincere Faith Knows the Source of Its Strength*

2 Corinthians 12:9

But he said to me, "My grace is sufficient for you, for my power is made perfect in weakness." Therefore I will boast all the more gladly about my weaknesses, so that Christ's power may rest on me.

---

8. *Sincere Faith Is Generous*

2 Corinthians 9:6–8

Remember this: Whoever sows sparingly will also reap sparingly, and whoever sows generously will also reap generously. Each man should give what he has decided in his heart to give, not reluctantly or under compulsion, for God loves a cheerful giver. And God is able to make all grace abound to you, so that in all things at all times, having all that you need, you will abound in every good work.

---

12. *Sincere Faith Examines Itself*

2 Corinthians 13:11

Finally, brothers, good-by. Aim for perfection, listen to my appeal, be of one mind, live in peace. And the God of love and peace will be with you.

---

9. *Sincere Faith Walks in Humility and Boldness*

2 Corinthians 10:4–5

The weapons we fight with are not the weapons of the world. On the contrary, they have divine power to demolish strongholds. We demolish arguments and every pretension that sets itself up against the knowledge of God, and we take captive every thought to make it obedient to Christ.